Published by Spines
ISBN 979-8-89569-899-0

"Through My Glasses: A Journey of Self-Love"
By Marquita Lawrence

To my beautiful daughters, **Arielle** and **Zuri,** who inspire me every day with their laughter, curiosity, and endless imaginations. You both are my guiding stars, lighting up my world and teaching me that true strength and beauty come from within. This book is a celebration of the unique and wonderful ways you both see the world, and I hope it reminds you, and every child who reads it, of how special and strong they are.

Thank you to everyone who believed in me and this story, helping to bring ***Through My Glasses: A Journey of Self-Love*** to life. Your support and encouragement lifted my spirits and gave me the courage to pursue this dream. To each person who pre-ordered, especially *Martrell Fisher-Smith, Nazinggar Harry, Janice Robinson, Vermeka Seymour,* and *Cheyennis Doom,* thank you for your faith in me and for cheering me on. This journey wouldn't have been the same without you.

May this book bring light, love, and confidence to every reader. It's dedicated to all who see the world a little differently and who know that beauty and strength come from embracing what makes us unique. Thank you for being a part of this story and for inspiring me to make it a reality.

Marquita Lawrence

Hi! My name is **Dion**, what's your name?

....

Wow! What a great name! It's really nice to meet you!

I notice that you wear glasses. I do too! But don't worry, wearing glasses may be scary at first, but really it isn't that bad at all. Maybe I'll share my story to help you feel a little better about wearing your glasses!

Oh, this is going to be great because it's the story of how my new glasses helped me see the world in amazing ways and feel proud of who I am! Let's explore together how seeing clearly can show us that being a little different is actually really, really cool."

What makes you special?

....

Write or draw it here!

A BLURRY START

Dion blinked hard, trying to make the fuzzy, smudged lines on the board come into focus. The chalk marks looked like melting clouds floating in and out of sight. No matter how she squinted, the words stayed a tangled blur. It felt like everyone else in class could see something she couldn't, like a secret only she was left out of."

"I wish I could see the board like everyone else... but all I see are fuzzy, wiggly lines! Thought Dion. "Hey! Can you read what that says? Mrs. Garcia wrote something funny on the board!" Her friend Chris asked. "Oh, um... I, uh... can't really see it today. My eyes are, um... just tired!" Dion pretended as she shyly turned away

Dion felt a little sad and embarrassed. It was hard to keep up with everyone, and every time she tried to squint, it just made things worse. The words danced farther and farther away, like they were playing a game she couldn't win.

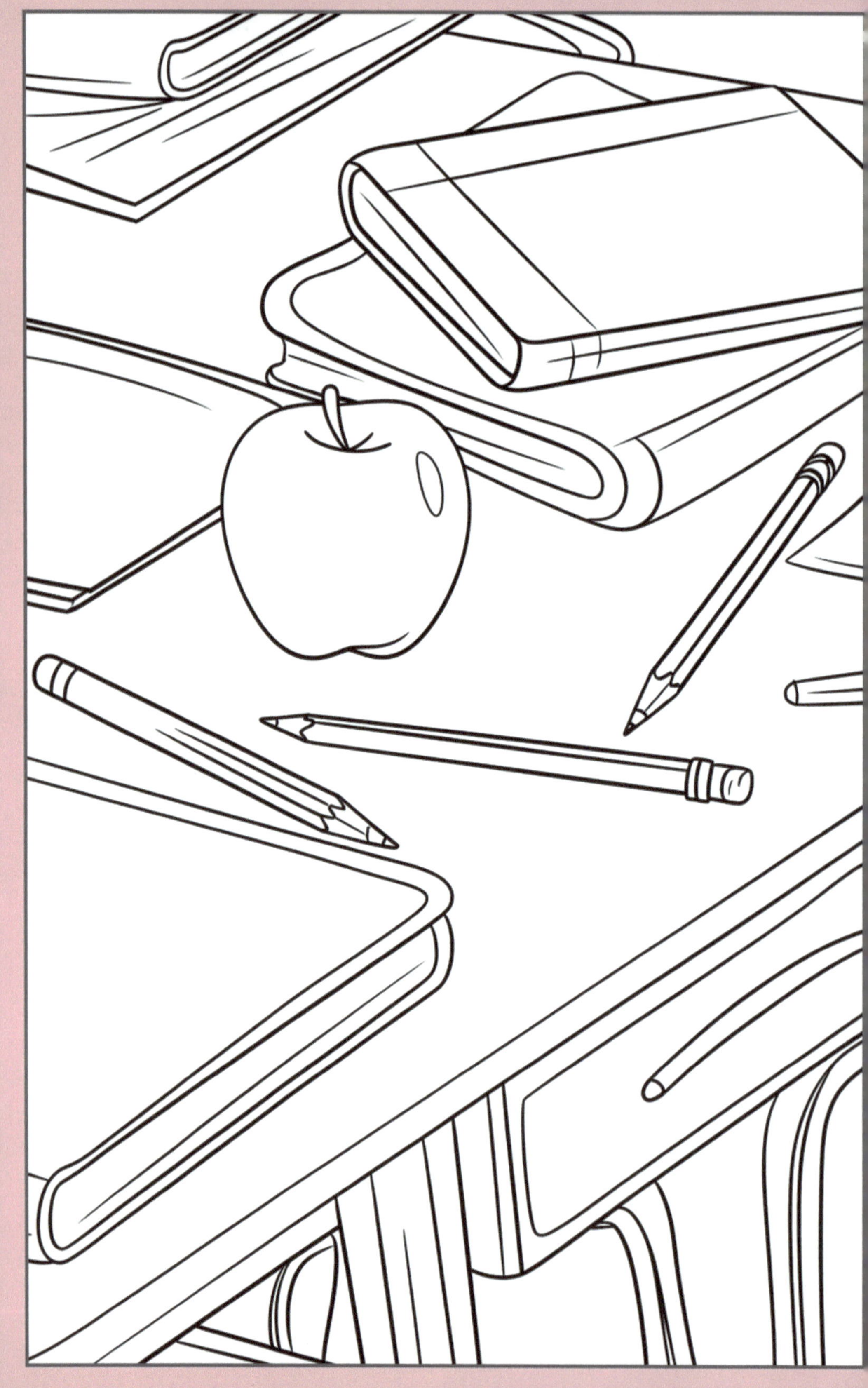

Have you ever felt left out?

Draw or write what happened and how it made you feel.

Missing Out on Fun

Later that day, Dion and her mom went to the park. The sun was shining bright, painting everything in warm, golden colors. Other kids were running and playing in the grass, and Dion could hear the chirps of birds high in the trees. But every time she looked up, it was like the branches and leaves melted into one fuzzy blob. She could barely make out the colors of flowers or see any details in the world around." "Want to go birdwatching, honey? Let's see if we can spot some cardinals!" Mom said. "Sure, Mom!" Replied Dion.

Walking along the park path a few minutes later, Dion found herself struggling to make something out of a tree. Squinting at a tree, she asks, "Mom, is that a bird... or a leaf?" Mom giggled and replied, "Sweetheart, that's a leaf... and it's close to falling!"

Dion felt a little embarrassed, as if the world was laughing quietly. All around were bright colors and clear shapes that she couldn't quite touch, like looking through a cloudy window. It was starting to feel lonely.

Although unsure of what it was exactly, her mom still sensed her fears and held her hand tightly to reassure her. Whispering to her daughter, she said: "Don't worry, everything will work out for good, but for now, let's go home."

Concerned Mom
Steps In

At home, Dion's mom watched with a gentle smile, always noticing the little things. She saw how Dion kept squinting, how she tilted her head just so, trying to get a better look at the world around her.

Honey, I noticed you were squinting a lot today. Are you having trouble seeing things?" Mom asked.

"Maybe a little, but... I don't want anyone to laugh at me." Dion hesitantly replied.
Mom hugged Dion tightly and said: "No one should ever make you feel bad about who you are. Let's get your eyes checked. A little extra help is nothing to be embarrassed about. Besides, you know your mom is blind as a bat, too."

Dion chuckled at her mom's silliness but also felt comforted as if a warm blanket had wrapped around her worries. Mom always knew how to make everything feel okay, like no problem was too big to handle together, and she noticed that she did all of that while wearing her own cute glasses to help her see clearly. "Maybe I can see the world glamorously like mommy one day." She thought to herself.

Write or draw someone who helps you when you're feeling worried.

"FRIENDS"
Special people who may help
when we are feeling worried.

Meeting the
Eye Doctor

The eye doctor's office was bright and full of colorful posters of eyes, eyeballs, and glasses. Dr. Lopez, the eye doctor, was a tall man with a big smile and a friendly laugh that made Dion feel like she was talking to a new friend.

"Hi there! I'm Dr. Lopez. Now, let's check those amazing eyes of yours. Ready for some magic?!" Dr. Lopez said excitedly.

"Magic? Like a spell?" Dion asked nervously. She couldn't understand why the doctor was so excited about her getting her eyes checked.

"Sort of! Watch this... can you read this line? Don't worry if it's fuzzy—it's all part of the magic!" Dr. Lopez said after giving her a reassuring eye wink.

Dr. Lopez's voice was like music, cheerful and gentle, making the tests feel more like a game. Soon, the tests were done, and Dion waited anxiously, fidgeting in the big doctor's chair.

"What would the eye doctor tell her next?" she thought.

"Looks like you have astigmatism and are a bit nearsighted. That just means your eyes need a little boost to see far away." Dr. Lopez said reassuringly.

"Really? So, what do I need to do?" asked Dion.

"Just get glasses! The fun part is, you get to pick any style you like; we have some glamorously fun ones right over here." Dr. Lopez said while walking them out of the dark eye testing room into the bright lobby.

E
F P
T O Z
L P E D D
P E C F D
E D F C Z P
F E L O P Z D
D E F P O T E C

E
F P
T O Z
L P E D
P E C F D
E D F C Z P
F E L O P Z D

Choosing Glasses

The glasses display was like a rainbow trapped behind glass, with rows of shiny, sparkly, and bold frames. Dion's eyes widened as she walked up and down the display, almost dizzy with excitement. There were glasses with blue frames, pink frames, round frames, and even some that sparkled like stars.

"Look at all these glasses, Dion! You can pick any color, any shape. What do you like?" asked Mom. Dion couldn't help but gasp with excitement. "Wow! There's one with sparkles! And this one is like a superhero mask!" she said excitedly.

"Let's see what fits your style the best. You're going to be the coolest kid around." Said Mom while giving her a wink of reassurance.

Finally, Dion picked a pair with just the right amount of sparkle, something that felt as bold as a superhero cape but comfortable enough to wear all day. They were perfect.

The Big Reveal

The day came, and her glasses were ready for pickup. She was so excited to see how they would feel on her that she kept rushing her mom to hurry before the eye doctor's office closed.

They finally got to the eye doctor, and the nice lady at the desk handed her the glasses in a cute, colorful case.

"I believe these are yours." The lady said kindly. As soon as Dion put on the new glasses, the world transformed. Everything was sharp, every color was rich, and even the tiniest details—like the creases on Mom's smile—were clear as crystal. She felt like seeing for the first time."

"Mom... everything looks like a painting! I can see every little thing!" She said with such tearful excitement.

"It's amazing, right? The world is so beautiful,

and you're going to see it all in a whole new way." Replied her Mom.

Dion looked around in awe. "I can see all the leaves! And the clouds are so... fluffy!" as she giggled and skipped outside the eye doctor's office.

First Day
back at School

The next day, Dion walked into school with a mixture of excitement and nerves. Butterflies danced in her stomach as she stepped into the classroom, secretly hoping that no one would laugh. She loved her glasses, but she was also the only one in her class that is now wearing them. "What would her classmates and friends think? Would they laugh?" she thought nervously to herself.

"Okay, here it goes... Just walk in and pretend you're a superhero..." she whispered to herself.

"Whoa, cool glasses! They're so sparkly!" her friend Chris said. He notices everything all the time.

Dion was relieved. "Thanks! They help me see like a superhero, too!" she said excitedly. Even though it was just one friend, Dion felt a rush of pride. Maybe being a little different wasn't so bad after all."

"Draw yourself with something that makes you feel proud!"

Embracing
the New View

At home that day, Dion decided to read a new book the Librarian had suggested a week before, but just wasn't able to read clearly at arm's length away. This time, reading her book was a little bit different.

"I didn't know this book had such clear pictures in the margins!" Dion said out loud to her mom

"See, honey? The world has been waiting for you to see it clearly; never be afraid to put your glasses on and See the World Glamorously!" replied her mom reassuringly. Her mom wanted her to know that wearing her glasses is a badge of honor because it helps her to be better than she was before. Dion was relieved: "Thanks, Mommy!" she said as her remaining bit of doubt started melting away.

With new confidence, Dion could finally enjoy things in ways that weren't possible before. Dion can finally See the World Glamorously through her new sparkly glasses.

"Draw yourself with your
new pair of glasses"

I hope my story has inspired you to always wear your glasses and never be afraid to see the world glamorously through your spectacles. If you don't have glasses but have any other physically unique trait that sets you apart from others, be proud of who you are. You can see the world glamorously, too, with your confidence and positive internal vision. Remember, your parents are there to help, so if you're having difficulty, go to them, I know they will do all they can to help you grow with confidence and a smile.

Anyway, that's all for now. Check out my tips on taking good care of your new glasses.

You have to make sure your superpower stays working after all.

Take Care of Your Superpower!

Glasses need a little care, just like a superhero's equipment! Here's a guide for keeping them in top shape.

1. Clean Your Glasses Every Day

* **Why?** Keeping lenses clean helps you see clearly and makes your glasses last longer.
* **How?** Gently wipe your glasses with a soft microfiber cloth. You can also use lens cleaner spray (ask a grown-up for help if needed). Avoid using tissues or your shirt to clean lenses, as these can scratch them.

2. Keep Glasses in a Safe Place

* **Why?** A safe spot protects your glasses from getting scratched or broken.
* **Where?** Always put your glasses in their case when you're not wearing them. If you're at school or somewhere else, try keeping them in a pocket in your backpack or on a safe shelf.

3. Hold Them Carefully

* **Why?** Grabbing glasses the right way keeps them from bending out of shape.
* **How?** Use both hands to put your glasses on or take them off. This keeps the frame balanced and prevents bending.

4. Avoid Putting Glasses on Your Head

* **Why?** Placing glasses on your head can stretch the frames and make them loose.
* **What to Do Instead?** If you need to take a quick break from wearing them, store them in your case or hang them around your neck with a strap.

5. Keep Them Dry

* **Why?** Water and high humidity can damage lenses and frames over time.
* **What to Do?** Take your glasses off if it's raining or if you're playing in the water. Dry them right away if they get wet.

6. Be Gentle with the Lenses

* **Why?** Scratches make it harder to see clearly.
* **How?** Avoid touching the lenses with your fingers, as oils can stick and make them smudgy. Handle your glasses by the frames.

7. Wear Your Glasses All Day (*Unless Told Otherwise*)

* **Why?** Consistently wearing your glasses helps your eyes adjust, letting you see clearly all the time.
* **When to Take Them Off?** Unless it's time for a nap, bath, or sports practice, where they could get damaged, keep your glasses on. They're there to help you see!

Daily Glasses Care Checklist

* Clean lenses with a soft microfiber cloth
* Store glasses in their case when not wearing them
* Use both hands to put on and take off glasses
* Avoid putting glasses on your head
* Dry glasses if they get wet
* Keep fingers off the lenses
* Wear glasses all day as advised

Bonus Tip: Remember to show off your glasses with confidence! They're a part of what makes you unique and ready to see the world glamorously!

"Check off each day to keep you glasses in tip-top shape!"

www.ingramcontent.com/pod-product-compliance
Lightning Source LLC
Chambersburg PA
CBHW040859110726
48005CB00001B/122